# THE SPACE RACE

# MISSILES AND SPY SATELLITES

### BY
## JOHN HAMILTON

**Abdo & Daughters**
An imprint of Abdo Publishing | abdobooks.com

**abdobooks.com**

Published by Abdo Publishing, a division of ABDO, PO Box 398166, Minneapolis, Minnesota 55439. Copyright © 2019 by Abdo Consulting Group, Inc. International copyrights reserved in all countries. No part of this book may be reproduced in any form without written permission from the publisher. Abdo & Daughters™ is a trademark and logo of Abdo Publishing.

Printed in the United States of America, North Mankato, Minnesota.
012019
012019

THIS BOOK CONTAINS
RECYCLED MATERIALS

**Editor:** Sue Hamilton
**Copy Editor:** Bridget O'Brien
**Graphic Design:** Sue Hamilton
**Cover Design:** Candice Keimig and Pakou Moua
**Cover Photo:** NASA
**Interior Images:** Getty-pgs 37, 38 & 39; Granger-pgs 23 & 40-41; iStock-pgs 26-27; The Image Works-pgs 7 & 9; NASA-pgs 4-5, 10 (bottom), 21 & 37 (left); Science Source-pgs 12-13, 24-25 & 33; Shutterstock-pg 9; Smithsonian Institution-pgs 8, 11 (top and bottom), 15, 18, 22 & 42; U.S. Air Force-pgs 29, 41 & 43; U.S. Navy-pg 32 (bottom); White House-pg 36; Wikimedia-pgs 10 (top right & left) & 16.

Library of Congress Control Number: 2018950001
Publisher's Cataloging-in-Publication Data
Names: Hamilton, John, author.
Title: Missiles and spy satellites / by John Hamilton.
Description: Minneapolis, Minnesota : Abdo Publishing, 2019 | Series: The space race | Includes online resources and index.
Identifiers: ISBN 9781532118302 (lib. bdg.) | ISBN 9781532171550 (ebook)
Subjects: LCSH: Spy satellites--Juvenile literature. | Intelligence satellites--Juvenile literature. | Guided missiles--Juvenile literature. | Space race--Juvenile literature.
Classification: DDC 629.4--dc23

# CONTENTS

# THE SPACE RACE

After World War II ended in 1945, two superpowers emerged: the United States and the Soviet Union. These two allies combined forces during the war to defeat the worldwide threat of Nazi Germany, Japan, and Italy. After the war, however, their partnership quickly fell apart.

Each side wanted to show the world that its system of government was best. The conquest of space was a perfect way to show off their superior technology. At first, the military drove the space race. Each side worked to build better rockets and missiles that could strike targets across the oceans. Spy satellites were sent into orbit so suspicious generals and politicians could keep an eye on the enemy.

With time, another goal arose. Both the United States and the Soviet Union vowed to put people into space. The ultimate goal: to land someone on the Moon.

## A RACE TO THE MOON

Apollo 11 launches on July 16, 1969. Astronauts Neil Armstrong, Buzz Aldrin, and Michael Collins sit atop the powerful Saturn V rocket, heading toward the Moon.

# EARLY ROCKETS

**M**odern rockets are powerful enough to send spacecraft billions of miles beyond the edge of our Solar System. The history of the Space Race, however, began hundreds of years ago, when rockets were simple toys.

Around 400 BC, a Greek man named Archytas lived in the southern city of Tarentum, Italy. He amused people by making a wooden pigeon "fly." Archytas partly filled the wooden bird with water and then

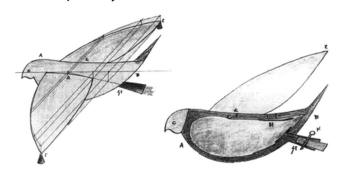

**ARCHYTAS' STEAM-POWERED PIGEON**

Archytas, a Greek inventor, developed a "flying" wooden pigeon around 400 BC. He used steam-power to launch the toy into the air.

heated it over a fire. The water turned to steam and shot out of a hole in the pigeon. The toy was then thrust in the opposite direction.

Three hundred years after Archytas, a Greek named Hero, from the city of Alexandria, invented another steam-powered curiosity. He mounted a sphere above a kettle of water. A fire under the kettle turned the water to steam. The steam forcefully escaped through two L-shaped tubes. This caused the sphere to rotate rapidly, to the amazement of everyone who saw it.

Nobody really knows when or where true rockets were invented. It probably happened somewhere in China during the first century AD. Chinese chemists experimented with early forms of gunpowder and used it to make fireworks. They made fireworks by putting the explosives in bamboo tubes. When set on fire, the escaping gasses from the gunpowder caused the tubes to fly through the air. The Chinese also attached the bamboo tubes to arrows. These solid-fuel "fire arrows" flew straighter than the bamboo rockets alone.

The first known use of rockets in warfare happened in 1232 at the Battle of Kai-Ken. The Chinese used masses of fire arrows to kill and frighten invaders from Mongolia.

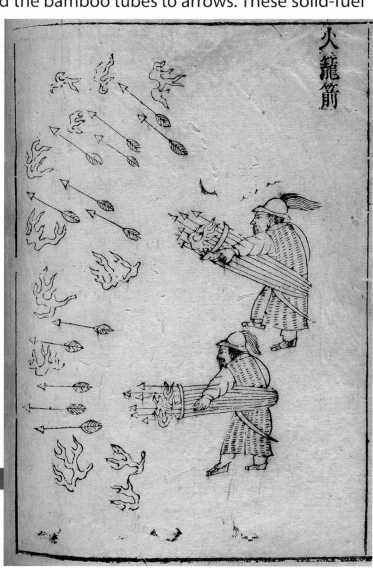

## FIRE ARROWS

Chinese warriors use "fire arrows" launched from bamboo tubes against their enemies.

# HOW ROCKETS WORK

Think of a rocket as if it were a balloon. First, you inflate it with air. When you squeeze shut the neck, or nozzle, there is a pressure inside the balloon. The pressure is higher than

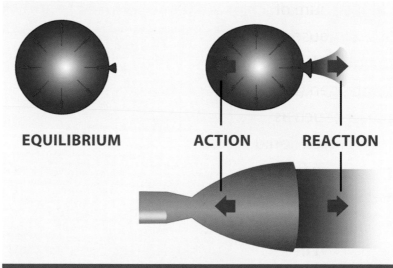

**EQUILIBRIUM**      **ACTION**      **REACTION**

### A BALLOON MIMICS A ROCKET'S PROPULSION

A balloon shows how rocket propulsion works. However, with balloons, the pressurized gas is the air trapped inside. With rockets, the pressurized gas is produced by burning propellants. These may be solid, liquid, or some of each.

the air outside. The balloon stays where it is because the air presses equally against the inside walls of the balloon. The pressure is the same in every direction.

When you let go of the nozzle, you create an imbalance in the balloon. The internal pressure at the front of the balloon is now greater than the pressure at the back. The air shoots out of the hole, and the balloon is thrust forward. This shows physicist Sir Isaac Newton's third law of motion: for every action in nature, there is an equal and opposite reaction.

Modern rockets use the same basic science as the balloon example. One big difference is that rockets get their thrust by burning fuel, such as liquid hydrogen. In order to burn something, you need oxygen. Normal jet engines get their oxygen from the air they fly through. Rockets can work in the vacuum of space because they carry their own oxygen (an oxidizer), such as super-cooled liquid oxygen. The fuel and oxidizer are mixed together and burned in a combustion chamber at the back of the rocket. The hot, pressurized gas spews out of the engine. Following Newton's third law of motion, the rocket then moves forward in the opposite direction.

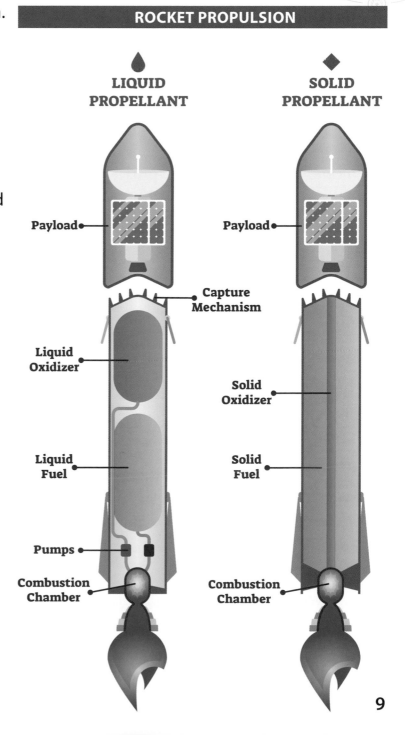

**ROCKET PROPULSION**

LIQUID PROPELLANT

SOLID PROPELLANT

Payload

Capture Mechanism

Liquid Oxidizer

Liquid Fuel

Pumps

Combustion Chamber

Payload

Solid Oxidizer

Solid Fuel

Combustion Chamber

# ROCKET PIONEERS

In 1865, French novelist Jules Verne (1801-1899) published the science fiction classic *From the Earth to the Moon*. Three adventurers climb inside a spacecraft shaped like a bullet and are shot out of an enormous cannon toward the Moon. Their story of exploration fired the public's imagination. Many wondered if rockets could be made that would really take astronauts into space.

One of those dreamers was a Russian schoolteacher named Konstantin Tsiolkovsky (1857-1935). He was a self-taught physicist and mathematician. In 1903, he published a scientific paper called *The Exploration of Cosmic Space by Means of Reaction Devices*. At a time when cars and airplanes had just been invented, Tsiolkovsky (Sil-kof-skee) correctly showed how rockets could be used to travel in space. He also described multistage rockets, air locks, and rockets propelled by liquid oxygen and hydrogen. Many of his ideas are used in spacecraft today.

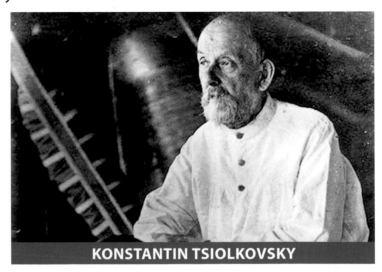

**KONSTANTIN TSIOLKOVSKY**

Another early rocket scientist was Romanian-born Hermann Oberth (1894-1989). In 1923, he published *The Rocket into Planetary Space*. He moved to Germany at age 18 and lived there the rest of his life. His work showed how powerful, multistage rockets could escape Earth's gravity.

HERMANN OBERTH

ROBERT GODDARD

Along with Tsiolkovsky and Oberth, American physicist Robert Goddard (1882-1945) is known today as one of the three fathers of modern rocketry. In 1926, he became the first person to successfully build and test a rocket using liquid fuel. He proved that rockets can work in the airless vacuum of space. He also invented ways to steer rockets in flight, and made pumps for rocket fuel. In honor of his pioneering work, NASA named Maryland's Goddard Space Flight Center after him.

# THE V-2 MISSILE

By the 1930s, many nations realized that rockets could be powerful weapons. Scientists worked to find ways to invent long-range missiles that could carry explosives and fly automatically.

One of the most terrifying weapons of World War II (1939-1945) was the German V-2 missile. First flown by the Nazis in 1942, the V-2 carried 2,000 pounds (907 kg) of explosives at targets about 200 miles (322 km) away. Using a potent mix of ethyl alcohol and liquid oxygen fuel, the V-2 became the first man-made object to reach space.

After launch, the 46-foot (14-m) -tall missile was guided to its target by gyroscopes and rudders. The V-2 was a ballistic missile. In other words, it was a gravity bomb. Once its fuel supply was cut off, it simply fell back to Earth, like a baseball that is hit into left field.

During World War II, the German military recruited a team of scientists to develop the V-2 missile. They were led by aerospace engineer Wernher von Braun (1912-1977). The missile was officially called the A-4 by the German military. However, it was widely known as the V-2. The "V" stood for a German word that means "vengeance weapon."

**CONCENTRATION CAMP LABOR**

Prisoners from the Mittelbau-Dora concentration camp were used as slave laborers to build German V-2s. They worked in a secret underground factory called Mittelwerk.

Von Braun and his team built and tested V-2 missiles on a German military base at Peenemünde, on the coast of the Baltic Sea. British bomber attacks forced the Germans to move farther inland. A secret underground factory called Mittelwerk was built near the town of Nordhausen. Slave workers from the Mittelbau-Dora concentration camp were used to make more than 5,000 V-2 missiles. The conditions in the tunnels were very harsh. Approximately 20,000 overworked prisoners died.

Germany began launching large numbers of V-2s in late 1944. Between September 1944 and March 1945, more than 2,900 missiles were fired at targets in England, France, and Belgium. The V-2 could cross the English Channel and strike London, England, in less than 5 minutes.

## V-2 WEAPON

The V-2 was used as a weapon of terror. It flew so high and fast that there was no warning, and no way to shoot it down (unlike the earlier, slower German V-1 "buzz bomb" missile). When it struck the ground, its payload of explosives ignited, strong enough to devastate an entire city block.

Buildings lie in ruins after the last V-2 missile of World War II hit East London on March 27, 1945.

Even though the V-2 could be destructive, the missile program as a whole was unsuccessful. About 7,000 people were killed by V-2s in Europe, but many more thousands died making them. The V-2's primitive guidance system caused it to often miss its target and explode harmlessly in the countryside. Also, each V-2 was extremely expensive to make, about the same as a fighter airplane. But the V-2 did limited damage, if it hit a target at all, and could only be used once.

Despite these problems, the V-2 was a breakthrough in missile design. Its guidance system was an important new technology that other countries wanted.

As the war came to an end in 1945, the V-2's lead scientist, Wernher von Braun, had a decision to make. He knew that the Americans, the British, and the Soviets wanted the plans to the V-2. Which side would he surrender to?

A cruise missile goes up during a ground-launched test at Dugway Proving Grounds in Utah.

## WHAT IS THE DIFFERENCE BETWEEN A ROCKET AND A MISSILE?

A very simple explanation is that rockets go straight in the direction they are pointed. Missiles are guided, usually by a computer or a sensor that steers it toward a target.

German V-2s used rocket engines that made the craft fly upwards. They also used gyroscopes and simple steering vanes that kept them on course toward a distant target. That made them early ground-to-ground missiles. Today, missiles can also detect heat, or other kinds of energy, to keep them on course. They can also be guided by lasers or satellites.

In simple military terms, a missile usually has a warhead that contains explosives, chemicals, or biological weapons. Rockets usually carry scientific instruments, or even astronauts. However, some rockets are guided, like missiles. It is confusing, and the two terms are often used together.

A Saturn V rocket sends Apollo 11 to the Moon.

# WERNHER VON BRAUN

When Wernher von Braun (1912-1977) grew up in Germany, his mother gave him a telescope. This made him excited to learn astronomy. Science fiction books by Jules Verne and H.G. Wells also fired his imagination.

As a young man, von Braun was influenced by the work of rocket scientist Hermann Oberth. Von Braun learned math and physics to better understand rocketry. He also joined a German rocket club called the Society for Space Travel.

The work of von Braun and his team of scientists came to the attention of the German military. In 1932, they went to work developing weapons for Adolf Hitler and the Nazis. It was a way for von Braun to invent different rocket designs.

Wernher von Braun was officially a Nazi, but he was more interested in space exploration.

**GERMAN ROCKET SCIENTISTS**

In the 1930s, Wernher von Braun was part of a famous group of rocket experimenters in Germany. He stands second from right in this photo.

He wanted the main goal of the V-2 program to be manned spaceflight. As World War II dragged on, however, von Braun realized his missiles would only be used as weapons of war by the Germans.

Wernher von Braun (center, without a military cap) stands with Nazi officials at an inspection of the testing and launching sites in Peenemünde, Germany. Von Braun must have known that his V-2s were being built by slave laborers, but he did nothing to stop the war crimes.

Von Braun is a controversial figure today. He surely knew that slave labor was being used to construct V-2 missiles. But by the time he was aware of these war crimes, could he do anything about it? Maybe he could have secretly sabotaged the missile program, or even fled Germany. However, von Braun was too blinded by his dream of spaceflight. He needed the German military to continue his research, and so he did nothing.

By 1945, the Germans had suffered many battlefield defeats. The war seemed lost. Von Braun knew that American and Soviet military forces were racing to capture V-2 rockets and plans. The Soviets had captured the German Peenemünde rocket launch site in the spring. Now they wanted to snatch the brains behind the missiles.

With American and Soviet forces driving deeper into Germany, von Braun and his team of scientists were shuttled from town to town. Their guards were ordered to execute them rather than allow them to be captured. As the war finally neared its end, the guards let many of the scientists roam freely.

In May 1945, von Braun surrendered to the American Army. It was his best chance to continue his rocket research. He also didn't want V-2 technology to fall into the hands of the Soviet government, which was run by the brutal dictator Joseph Stalin.

## V-2 IN THE USA

A V-2 rocket is launched at White Sands Proving Ground in New Mexico on September 2, 1948. Wernher von Braun surrendered to U.S. soldiers in May 1945. He and members of his team helped Americans assemble and launch captured V-2 rockets.

Dr. von Braun became the first director of NASA's Marshall Space Flight Center.

The U.S. Army had a plan called Operation Paperclip. It secretly sent German rocket scientists and V-2 parts back to America. Von Braun and about 125 of his rocketry team worked for the Army at Fort Bliss, Texas. They designed new rockets. They also helped teach American scientists how to assemble and launch captured V-2 rockets at the nearby White Sands Proving Ground (later called the White Sands Missile Range) in New Mexico. They later worked at the Army's Redstone Arsenal near Huntsville, Alabama, and were eventually transferred to NASA's Marshall Space Flight Center. Von Braun became the center's first director.

During his long career, Wernher von Braun and his team helped design many rockets and missiles. They included the Redstone rocket, the Jupiter missile, the Pershing missile, as well as the Saturn rockets that took American astronauts to the Moon.

# SERGEI KOROLEV

**YOUNG ROCKET SCIENTISTS**

Russian rocket engineers and enthusiasts pose with their first liquid-fuel rocket, GIRD-X, in 1933. In Russian, GIRD stands for Group for the Study of Reactive Motion. At far left, in a Red Army cap, is Sergei Korolev.

Near the end of World War II in 1945, as the Soviet Red Army swept through eastern Germany, it captured every rocket scientist it could find. The Soviets were eager to learn their secrets. The big prize, however, was top German rocket designer Wernher von Braun and his team of engineers. But they had already been snatched up by the Americans. The Soviets would have to find someone else to help them build better rockets.

As a young man growing up in the 1910s and 1920s, Sergei Korolev (1906-1966) fell in love with airplanes. He studied aeronautical engineering and designed gliders and other aircraft. He earned a pilot's license, and then became fascinated with space travel after studying the work of Russian rocket pioneer Konstantin Tsiolkovsky. Korolev became a very talented and hardworking rocket designer.

The Soviet military became interested in Korolev's experiments with liquid-fueled rockets. He worked for the government designing rockets that could carry weapons or people into space.

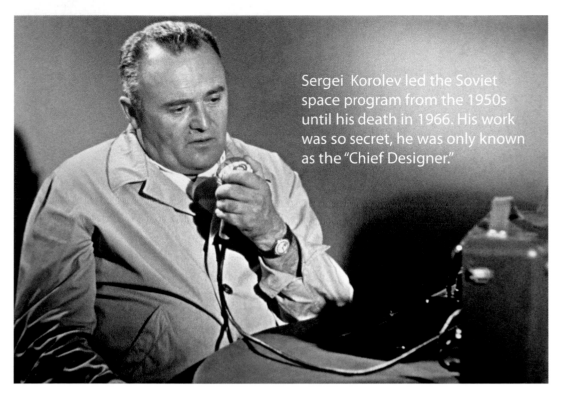

Sergei Korolev led the Soviet space program from the 1950s until his death in 1966. His work was so secret, he was only known as the "Chief Designer."

In 1938, Korolev was falsely accused by the Soviet Union of sabotaging the government's rocket program. This was part of the Soviet Union's "Great Terror." Millions of people suspected of being enemies of the government were killed or imprisoned. Korolev was tortured and exiled to faraway Siberia.

When World War II ended in 1945, the Soviet Union realized it needed rocket designers to help it understand captured German V-2s. Korolev was released and ordered to study the V-2. He worked with captured German rocket engineers as well as Soviet scientists.

In the coming years, Korolev became a colonel in the Red Army, and the head rocket and spacecraft engineer of the Soviet Union. His identity was kept top secret. To the outside world, he was known only as the "Chief Designer." He was responsible for many long-range Soviet missiles, satellites, and manned spacecraft. It was only after Korolev's death in 1966 that his true identity was revealed as the most important Soviet rocket designer of the Space Race.

# THE COLD WAR

The democratic United States and the communist Soviet Union had very different kinds of governments. They distrusted each other. They competed in many ways, especially with their militaries. Without actually going to war against each other, they spent vast amounts of money to develop new and powerful weapons. This "Cold War" saw competition in unexpected places, including space.

Out of the ashes of World War II, the United States and the Soviet Union emerged as the world's two superpowers. During the war, they seemed to be equals. But in 1945, the United States used nuclear bombs against Japan. These frightening weapons tipped the balance of power. After the war, Soviet leader Joseph Stalin was determined to get nuclear bombs for his own country, and find ways to fire them quickly across the oceans. The Soviets detonated their first nuclear bomb in 1949. People in the United States were shocked. Next would come a race in missile technology between the two countries, and a race into space to show the world once and for all which country was the most powerful.

The first U.S. atom bomb test took place near Alamogordo, New Mexico, on July 16, 1945.

# THE ICBM

In the opening days of the Cold War, both the United States and the Soviet Union had nuclear bombs. They were the most fearsome, destructive weapons ever invented. The next step was to find a way to drop the bombs on the enemy in the quickest, most devastating way possible.

Building on the success of the German V-2, each country worked hard to improve its missile technology. They wanted a way to drop a nuclear warhead anywhere in the world. They also wanted to strike so quickly that the enemy had no time to defend itself or strike back.

The militaries of both the United States and the Soviet Union realized that learning to travel in space would help them reach their goals. What they raced to build were powerful new missiles called ICBMs.

## A NUCLEAR STRIKE FROM SPACE

The illustration at right shows several intercontinental ballistic missiles (ICBMs) about to strike a distant target. In reality, the missiles would not be grouped so tightly together. Also, only the nuclear warheads at the top of the missiles would be falling toward the target. The speed of some modern ICBM warheads as they fall to Earth is more than 15 times the speed of sound.

ICBM stands for "intercontinental ballistic missile." "Intercontinental" means it can travel into space and then strike a faraway continent. For example, an ICBM launched from Asia could strike North America. "Ballistic" means that once the warhead is released, it falls back to Earth using gravity, like a ball tossed to the ground from a tall building. Modern ICBMs have a minimum range of about 3,400 miles (5,472 km).

The world's first ICBM came from the Soviet Union. It was the R-7 Semyorka, which was designed by the Soviet's chief rocket scientist Sergei Korolev. It was

**R-7 INTERCONTINENTAL BALLISTIC MISSILE LAUNCH**

The Soviet Union's R-7 was first successfully launched in 1957.

first successfully launched in 1957. It could deliver a single nuclear bomb up to 5,500 miles (8,851 km) away. It was 112 feet (34 m) tall. It used liquid-fuel engines, including four boosters strapped around a larger, central rocket. The R-7's basic design is still used today.

ICBM research started later in the United States than in the Soviet Union. The American military believed it could handle any threat with its fleet of long-range bomber aircraft. Making new missiles wasn't a top priority. That changed in the early 1950s when the Soviet Union exploded its first atomic bombs. The American military raced to catch up.

The first American ICBM was the Atlas missile. Its first successful flight was in 1958. The Atlas was 85 feet (26 m) tall. Like the Soviet R-7, its engine was powered by liquid fuel. It could strike a target up to 9,000 miles (14,484 km) away with its single nuclear warhead.

Research and testing of military missiles later helped human space exploration. Powerful ICBMs were sometimes used in manned spaceflight missions. Instead of carrying bombs, they were modified to carry capsules with astronauts or cosmonauts riding inside.

Soviet cosmonaut Yuri Gagarin, the first human to travel into space and orbit the Earth, was carried aloft by an R-7-style rocket. And astronaut Alan Shepard, the first American in space, rode a modified military Redstone missile that boosted his Mercury spacecraft into the history books.

The launch of a U.S. Air Force Atlas missile on February 20, 1958.

# SPUTNIK

**M**any history books mark October 4, 1957, as the beginning of the Space Race. On that date in the Soviet Union, a mighty R-7 rocket, designed by Sergei Korolev, rode a fireball into the night sky. When it reached the edges of space, instead of dropping a bomb, it released a beach-ball-sized metal sphere with four long antennas.

The mysterious object was called Sputnik 1. It was the first satellite made by humans to orbit the Earth. Sputnik 1 was an artificial moon. Its name translated to "fellow traveler."

The Soviet Union kept Sputnik 1's launch a secret. When the Soviet government revealed its presence, people were shocked, especially in the United States. The small satellite weighed 184 pounds (83 kg) and measured about 23 inches (58 cm) in diameter. It traveled around the Earth every 98 minutes, broadcasting a simple beeping radio signal as it sped along its elliptical orbit.

The Soviets had beaten the Americans into space and into Earth orbit. But how could such a small, beeping object cause such fear?

## SPUTNIK 1

The Soviet Union successfully launched Sputnik 1 on October 4, 1957. The small unmanned space satellite transmitted a radio signal for 22 days.

Two years before Sputnik was launched, in 1955, President Dwight Eisenhower announced that the United States would take part in a scientific event called the International Geophysical Year. It was to be an 18-month project from 1957 to 1958.

Scientists from more than 60 countries would exchange ideas and research. President Eisenhower said that the United States would contribute by launching the world's first Earth-orbiting satellite. It would be used for peaceful, scientific research. It would also show the world the superior technology of the United States.

German missile designer Wernher von Braun, who now worked for the U.S. government, was happy with the news. He and his team had been working on a new rocket called Redstone. It was very powerful, and could easily boost a satellite into Earth orbit.

Unfortunately for Wernher von Braun, his Redstone rocket was rejected. Instead, the U.S. Navy's Vanguard rocket was chosen to hoist the first American satellite into orbit.

**VANGUARD**

The U.S. Navy's Vanguard rocket was chosen to hoist the first American satellite into orbit in 1957. This photo shows a crane placing a Vanguard's first stage into position.

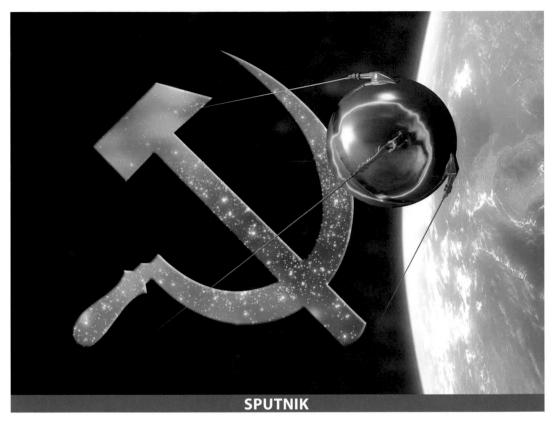

**SPUTNIK**

Rocket designer Sergei Korolev convinced Soviet leader Nikita Khrushchev that the Soviet Union had the technology to be the first country to launch a satellite into space. They did not wait for the United States, whose Vanguard rocket was not ready.

Meanwhile, in the Soviet Union, rocket designer Sergei Korolev argued that his country should also launch a satellite, and do it before the United States. Soviet leader Nikita Khrushchev agreed that such a project would prove that the Soviet Union, not America, was superior.

By 1957, the U.S. Vanguard rocket was far behind schedule. Wernher von Braun pleaded with the government to launch a satellite with his Redstone rocket, but his proposal was rejected. While the Americans delayed, the Soviets were ready to shock the world.

On October 4, 1957, the Soviet Union launched Sputnik 1 into orbit. It was stunning news around the world. This was a time when people in the United States and many other countries were suspicious of the Soviet Union. Until this time, most people were sure the United States was the most advanced country on Earth. But Sputnik 1 gave astonishing proof that the Soviets were just as technologically advanced, maybe even more so. Any ham radio operator could hear Sputnik 1's "beep … beep … beep" when it sailed overhead. People could also simply look up with binoculars or a telescope and see the shiny silver ball as it moved across the night sky.

Sputnik 1 launches
on October 4, 1957.

Some Americans looked up at Sputnik 1 in wonder. Astronauts Alan Shepard and Deke Slayton, as well as spacecraft designer Harrison Storms, were inspired to pursue careers in space exploration.

On November 3, 1957, the Soviets amazed the world again. Sputnik 2 was successfully launched into orbit. This time, the satellite carried several scientific instruments, as well as a dog named Laika. The Soviets proved that a living creature could survive being launched into space (although Laika died a few hours later).

Many Americans were fearful. Now that the Soviets had put the first satellites into orbit, what would they do next? Could they use satellites to spy on the United States? Could they even drop nuclear bombs down on unsuspecting American cities? The Space Race had suddenly become very real and very serious.

### SPACE DOG

On November 3, 1957, the Russian dog Laika became the first animal to orbit the Earth. She flew aboard Sputnik 2 and proved that a living creature could survive being launched into space.

# AMERICA'S TURN

The United States government was caught off guard by the Soviet Union's "October Surprise." The Sputnik 1 and Sputnik 2 satellites were stunning scientific achievements. They were also frightening reminders of how quickly the Soviet Union had become a real superpower capable of attacking the United States. The American public was frightened, and demanded to know why the United States had fallen so far behind its Cold War rival in science and technology. How long would it be before the Soviets launched a surprise nuclear attack on the United States? Could America ever catch up in the Space Race?

President Eisenhower ordered the Navy to launch a satellite on its Vanguard rocket as soon as possible. He wanted to calm fearful Americans and reassure them that the United States continued to have the best technology. The launch would even be shown on television.

## THE RUSH TO REASSURE

Eisenhower ordered the launch of a U.S. satellite on a Vanguard rocket.

On December 6, 1957, the Vanguard rocket lifted off from its launchpad at Florida's Cape Canaveral. Unfortunately, the launch did not go as planned. The 75-foot (23-m) tall, 3-stage rocket rose a few inches and then seemed to hover in the air for a moment. It finally sank back to Earth and exploded in an enormous fireball. The satellite was ejected from the top of the rocket and landed in some nearby bushes. Though damaged, it began to forlornly transmit its radio signals.

Vanguard explodes.

After the embarrassment of the Vanguard rocket's failure, the United States needed a "win" in the Space Race. Wernher von Braun's Redstone rocket was deemed America's best chance to catch up to the Soviet Union.

The Vanguard rocket failure was a terrible embarrassment to the United States. The country's space program seemed to be a mess compared to the Soviet Union. People were losing confidence in the government. After Vanguard's launchpad explosion, newspaper headlines across the country screamed "Flopnik!" and "Kaputnik!" At last, the government realized that Wernher von Braun's Redstone rocket was America's best chance to catch up to the Soviets. Von Braun and his team of scientists were ordered to prepare for launch.

The Redstone was a 69-foot (21-m) -tall, single-stage rocket. It was designed to be used by the military. Its main job was to carry nuclear weapons. On January 31, 1958, a modified Redstone perched on a launchpad at Florida's Cape Canaveral. The modified version was called Juno 1. Instead of carrying a nuclear bomb, it held a satellite called Explorer 1.

When the countdown clock reached zero, the Juno 1 rocket lifted off on a pillar of fire. The launch was flawless. Once it reached space, Explorer 1 was successfully released. America had finally put an artificial satellite into orbit around the Earth. Explorer 1 contained several scientific instruments. Some searched for cosmic radiation. The Explorer program eventually discovered the Van Allen Belts, which are large zones of radioactive particles that circle the Earth.

The Soviet Sputnik crisis resulted in many changes in the United States. New satellites were launched, and math and science were given more importance in schools. The U.S. government also put more effort into space exploration. On October 1, 1958, the National Aeronautics and Space Administration (NASA) was created. It took over for the old National Advisory Committee for Aeronautics (NACA). NASA would be responsible for all civilian space programs. The country's space exploration efforts would be more unified and streamlined. With any luck, the United States would keep up with, and maybe even outshine, its Cold War rival the Soviet Union.

# HIGH-FLYING SPIES

**L**aunching nuclear missiles or scientific satellites were not the only reasons to explore space. The United States military had another very important goal: to spy on the Soviet Union and other countries from high above.

Spy satellites, also called reconnaissance satellites, are used by the military to observe an enemy's bases, cities, and armed forces. This can be extremely useful when planning for war. It also helps the government decide how much money to spend on military equipment in order to respond to an enemy threat.

In the late 1950s, the Air Force's U-2 spy plane was used to take pictures of the Soviet Union's military forces. It flew at an altitude of 70,000 feet (21,336 m), which was too high to be shot down. But by 1960, the Soviets invented new missiles that could reach the high-flying U-2.

On May 1, 1960, a U-2 piloted by Captain Francis Gary Powers was shot down over the Soviet Union. Powers worked for the U.S. Central Intelligence Agency (CIA). His capture by the Soviets created an international crisis.

Powers was eventually set free. But even before the crisis began, the United States knew it needed a better way to keep track of the Soviet military. With the Space Race already begun, the military found what it was looking for: spy satellites.

**U-2 PILOT SHOT DOWN**

Captain Powers stands by his U-2 plane. He was shot down by the Soviets on May 1, 1960, causing an international crisis.

Corona, the first United States reconnaissance satellite.

Shortly after the Soviet Union launched Sputnik 1 in 1958, U.S. President Dwight Eisenhower signed an order that created a top-secret program. It would be run by the CIA and the Air Force. Its mission was to launch satellites that could take photographs of Soviet military bases and other targets. The photographs would then be retrieved after landing back on Earth in a heat-shielded capsule. The spy satellites were named Corona (code-named Discoverer).

Most Corona satellite cameras used black-and-white film. Each satellite could carry thousands of feet of film. On early missions, the cameras could see objects on the ground that were about 40 feet (12 m) across or bigger. As technology got better, the cameras were designed to detect objects as small as 3 feet (.9 m) in diameter.

The first successful Corona satellite was launched in August 1960. For the next 12 years, more than 100 Corona missions were flown. Combined, they took more than 800,000 photographs of the Soviet Union, China, and other hostile countries. The first photograph from space of Soviet territory revealed an air base in Siberia. That same mission revealed more territory in the Soviet Union than all the U-2 spy planes combined.

When a Corona mission was complete, the nose cone of the satellite was ejected and a return capsule fell to Earth. A shield protected the film from the intense heat of reentry through the atmosphere. A radio signal told operators its location. As the capsule neared the surface, a parachute was released. A special recovery aircraft swooped in and snatched the capsule out of midair.

**MID-AIR RECOVERY**

On August 18, 1960, a U.S. Air Force plane recovered the Corona capsule in midair over the Pacific Ocean. It was the first time any airplane had ever recovered a satellite data capsule in flight.

The Corona program was very effective. It helped the United States discover a great deal about the Soviet military. In the late 1950s, Americans feared there was a "missile gap" between the two counties. The Soviets were believed to have a far greater number of missiles than the United States. The Corona spy satellites proved that the opposite was true: the United States had more missiles. This knowledge helped ease the fear of a surprise Soviet missile attack.

# TIMELINE

**1926**—American scientist Robert Goddard becomes the first person to build and test a rocket using liquid fuel.

**1939, September 1**—World War II begins with Germany's invasion of Poland.

**1942**—German scientist Wernher von Braun builds and launches the first V-2 missile for Nazi Germany's war effort. Over the next three years, thousands of V-2s will be built by slave laborers from concentration camps.

**1945**—Wernher von Braun surrenders to American soldiers. World War II ends. Dr. von Braun and about 125 of his associates go to Fort Bliss, Texas, to build missiles for the United States.

**1950**—Dr. von Braun and his team go to the Redstone Arsenal near Huntsville, Alabama. They will design the U.S. Army's Redstone and Jupiter ballistic missiles, as well as the Jupiter C, Juno II, and Saturn I launch vehicles.

**1955**—President Dwight Eisenhower announces that the United States will attempt to launch the world's first artificial satellite to orbit the Earth during the upcoming International Geophysical Year in 1957-58. Soon after Eisenhower's announcement, Premier Nikita Khrushchev announces that the Soviet Union will also attempt to launch a satellite.

**1957, August 21**—The first successful flight of the Soviet R-7 Semyorka, the world's first intercontinental ballistic missile (ICBM).

**1957, October 4**—The Soviet Union launches the Sputnik 1 satellite. It marks the unofficial start of the space race.

**1957, November 3**—The Soviet Union launches Sputnik 2 into orbit. It contains various scientific instruments, plus a dog named Laika.

**1957, December 6**—The American Vanguard rocket explodes on the launchpad.

**1958, January 31**—The United States launches Explorer 1, the first American satellite launched into space.

**1958, October 1**—NASA (National Aeronautics and Space Administration), a U.S. government agency, officially begins work. Its original primary objective is to create Saturn rockets to fly to the Moon.

**1958, November 28**—The United States makes its first successful launch of an Atlas intercontinental ballistic missile (ICBM).

**1960**—Von Braun becomes director of NASA's Marshall Space Flight Center and the chief architect of the Saturn V launch vehicle.

**1960, August**—The first successful launch of a Corona reconnaissance satellite.

# GLOSSARY

### ASTRONAUT
Someone who travels in a spacecraft. The word has Greek roots that stand for "star sailor" or "star traveller."

### COLD WAR
The Cold War was a time of political, economic, and cultural tension between the United States and its allies and the Soviet Union and other Communist nations. It lasted from about 1947, just after the end of World War II, until the early 1990s, when the Soviet Union collapsed and Communism was no longer a major threat to the United States.

### COSMONAUT
An astronaut from Russia or the former Soviet Union.

### GYROSCOPE
A mechanical device often used in aircraft and spacecraft that provide stability and navigation.

### NATIONAL AERONAUTICS AND SPACE ADMINISTRATION (NASA)
A United States government space agency started in 1958. NASA's goals include space exploration and increasing people's understanding of Earth, our solar system, and the universe.

### ORBIT
The circular path a moon or spacecraft makes when traveling around a planet or other large celestial body.

### PAYLOAD

Something that is carried by an aircraft, rocket, or missile. Rockets can carry bombs, satellites, or spacecraft containing human astronauts or cosmonauts.

### SOVIET UNION

A former country that included a union of Russia and several other Communist republics. It was formed in 1922 and existed until 1991.

### VAN ALLEN BELTS

Zones of radioactive charged particles, shaped like huge donuts, that encircle the Earth. Most of the particles come from the solar wind and are captured by Earth's magnetic field. They are named for Dr. James Van Allen, a space scientist who worked at the University of Iowa. His instruments aboard the Explorer 1 and 3 satellites first proved the existence of the radiation belts.

### WARHEAD

Usually an explosive, a warhead is a kind of bomb that is sent to its target by a missile or rocket. Instead of explosives, some warheads carry toxic chemicals or harmful germs.

# ONLINE RESOURCES

**Booklinks**
**NONFICTION NETWORK**
FREE! ONLINE NONFICTION RESOURCES

To learn more about missiles and spy satellites, visit **abdobooklinks.com** or scan this QR code. These links are routinely monitored and updated to provide the most current information available.

# INDEX